Recipe:

Rating: ☆☆☆☆☆ Difficulty: ☆☆☆☆☆ Prep Time: Cook Time:

Ingredients:

Cooking Instructions:

Thoughts and Notes:

Recipe:

Rating: ☆☆☆☆☆ Difficulty: ☆☆☆☆☆ Prep Time: Cook Time:

Ingredients:

Cooking Instructions:

Thoughts and Notes:

Recipe:

Rating: ☆☆☆☆☆ Difficulty: ☆☆☆☆☆ Prep Time: _____ Cook Time: _____

Ingredients:

_____

_____

_____

_____

_____

Cooking Instructions:

_____

_____

_____

_____

_____

_____

_____

_____

_____

Thoughts and Notes:

_____

_____

_____

_____

Recipe:

Rating: ☆☆☆☆☆ Difficulty: ☆☆☆☆☆ Prep Time: Cook Time:

Ingredients:

Cooking Instructions:

Thoughts and Notes:

Recipe:

Rating: ☆☆☆☆☆ Difficulty: ☆☆☆☆☆ Prep Time: Cook Time:

Ingredients:

Cooking Instructions:

Thoughts and Notes:

Recipe:

Rating: ☆☆☆☆☆ Difficulty: ✿✿✿✿✿ Prep Time: Cook Time:

Ingredients:

Cooking Instructions:

Thoughts and Notes:

Recipe:

Rating: ☆☆☆☆☆ Difficulty: ☆☆☆☆☆ Prep Time: Cook Time:

Ingredients:

Cooking Instructions:

Thoughts and Notes:

Recipe:

Rating: ☆☆☆☆☆ Difficulty: ☆☆☆☆☆ Prep Time:　　　　Cook Time:

Ingredients:

Cooking Instructions:

Thoughts and Notes:

Recipe:

Rating: ☆☆☆☆☆ Difficulty: ✿✿✿✿✿ Prep Time: Cook Time:

Ingredients:

Cooking Instructions:

Thoughts and Notes:

Recipe:

Rating: ☆☆☆☆☆ Difficulty: ☆☆☆☆☆ Prep Time: Cook Time:

Ingredients:

Cooking Instructions:

Thoughts and Notes:

Recipe:

Rating: ☆☆☆☆☆ Difficulty: ☆☆☆☆☆ Prep Time: Cook Time:

Ingredients:

Cooking Instructions:

Thoughts and Notes:

Recipe:

Rating: ☆☆☆☆☆ Difficulty: ✿✿✿✿✿ Prep Time: Cook Time:

Ingredients:

Cooking Instructions:

Thoughts and Notes:

Recipe:

Rating: ☆☆☆☆☆ Difficulty: ✿✿✿✿✿ Prep Time: Cook Time:

Ingredients:

Cooking Instructions:

Thoughts and Notes:

Recipe:

Rating: ☆☆☆☆☆ Difficulty: ☆☆☆☆☆ Prep Time:

Cook Time:

Ingredients:

Cooking Instructions:

Thoughts and Notes:

Recipe:

Rating: ☆☆☆☆☆ Difficulty: ☆☆☆☆☆ Prep Time: Cook Time:

Ingredients:

Cooking Instructions:

Thoughts and Notes:

Recipe:

Rating: ☆☆☆☆☆ Difficulty: ✿✿✿✿✿ Prep Time:　　　　　Cook Time:

Ingredients:

Cooking Instructions:

Thoughts and Notes:

Recipe:

Rating: ☆☆☆☆☆ Difficulty: ☆☆☆☆☆ Prep Time: Cook Time:

Ingredients:

Cooking Instructions:

Thoughts and Notes:

Recipe:

Rating: ☆☆☆☆☆ Difficulty: ☆☆☆☆☆ Prep Time: Cook Time:

Ingredients:

Cooking Instructions:

Thoughts and Notes:

Recipe:

Rating: ☆☆☆☆☆ Difficulty: ✿✿✿✿✿ Prep Time: Cook Time:

Ingredients:

Cooking Instructions:

Thoughts and Notes:

Recipe:

Rating: ☆☆☆☆☆ Difficulty: ☆☆☆☆☆ Prep Time: Cook Time:

Ingredients:

Cooking Instructions:

Thoughts and Notes:

Recipe:

Rating: ☆☆☆☆☆ Difficulty: ☆☆☆☆☆ Prep Time: Cook Time:

Ingredients:

Cooking Instructions:

Thoughts and Notes:

Recipe:

Rating: ☆☆☆☆☆ Difficulty: ☆☆☆☆☆ Prep Time: Cook Time:

Ingredients:

Cooking Instructions:

Thoughts and Notes:

Recipe:

Rating: ☆☆☆☆☆ Difficulty: ☆☆☆☆☆ Prep Time: Cook Time:

Ingredients:

Cooking Instructions:

Thoughts and Notes:

Recipe:

Rating: ☆☆☆☆☆ Difficulty: ☆☆☆☆☆ Prep Time: Cook Time:

Ingredients:

Cooking Instructions:

Thoughts and Notes:

Recipe:

Rating: ☆☆☆☆☆ Difficulty: ☆☆☆☆☆ Prep Time: Cook Time:

Ingredients:

Cooking Instructions:

Thoughts and Notes:

Recipe:

Rating: ☆☆☆☆☆ Difficulty: ☆☆☆☆☆ Prep Time: Cook Time:

Ingredients:

Cooking Instructions:

Thoughts and Notes:

Recipe:

Rating: ☆☆☆☆☆ Difficulty: ☆☆☆☆☆ Prep Time: Cook Time:

Ingredients:

Cooking Instructions:

Thoughts and Notes:

Recipe:

Rating: ☆☆☆☆☆ Difficulty: ☆☆☆☆☆ Prep Time: Cook Time:

Ingredients:

Cooking Instructions:

Thoughts and Notes:

Recipe:

Rating: ☆☆☆☆☆ Difficulty: ✿✿✿✿✿ Prep Time: Cook Time:

Ingredients:

Cooking Instructions:

Thoughts and Notes:

Recipe:

Rating: ☆☆☆☆☆ Difficulty: ☆☆☆☆☆ Prep Time: Cook Time:

Ingredients:

Cooking Instructions:

Thoughts and Notes:

Recipe:

Rating: ☆☆☆☆☆ Difficulty: ☆☆☆☆☆ Prep Time: Cook Time:

Ingredients:

Cooking Instructions:

Thoughts and Notes:

Recipe:

Rating: ☆☆☆☆☆ Difficulty: ☆☆☆☆☆ Prep Time: Cook Time:

Ingredients:

Cooking Instructions:

Thoughts and Notes:

Recipe:

Rating: ☆☆☆☆☆ Difficulty: ✿✿✿✿✿ Prep Time: Cook Time:

Ingredients:

Cooking Instructions:

Thoughts and Notes:

Recipe:

Rating: ☆☆☆☆☆ Difficulty: ☆☆☆☆☆ Prep Time: Cook Time:

Ingredients:

Cooking Instructions:

Thoughts and Notes:

Recipe:

Rating: ☆☆☆☆☆ Difficulty: ☆☆☆☆☆ Prep Time: Cook Time:

Ingredients:

Cooking Instructions:

Thoughts and Notes:

Recipe:

Rating: ☆☆☆☆☆ Difficulty: ✿✿✿✿✿ Prep Time:

Cook Time:

Ingredients:

Cooking Instructions:

Thoughts and Notes:

Recipe:

Rating: ☆☆☆☆☆ Difficulty: ☆☆☆☆☆ Prep Time: Cook Time:

Ingredients:

Cooking Instructions:

Thoughts and Notes:

Recipe:

Rating: ☆☆☆☆☆ Difficulty: ☆☆☆☆☆ Prep Time: Cook Time:

Ingredients:

Cooking Instructions:

Thoughts and Notes:

Recipe:

Rating: ☆☆☆☆☆ Difficulty: ✿✿✿✿✿ Prep Time: Cook Time:

Ingredients:

Cooking Instructions:

Thoughts and Notes:

Recipe:

Rating: ☆☆☆☆☆ Difficulty: ☆☆☆☆☆ Prep Time: Cook Time:

Ingredients:

Cooking Instructions:

Thoughts and Notes:

Recipe:

Rating: ☆☆☆☆☆ Difficulty: ☆☆☆☆☆ Prep Time: Cook Time:

Ingredients:

Cooking Instructions:

Thoughts and Notes:

Recipe:

Rating: ☆☆☆☆☆ Difficulty: ☆☆☆☆☆ Prep Time: Cook Time:

Ingredients:

Cooking Instructions:

Thoughts and Notes:

Recipe:

Rating: ☆☆☆☆☆ Difficulty: ☆☆☆☆☆ Prep Time: Cook Time:

Ingredients:

Cooking Instructions:

Thoughts and Notes:

Recipe:

Rating: ☆☆☆☆☆ Difficulty: ✿✿✿✿✿ Prep Time: Cook Time:

Ingredients:

Cooking Instructions:

Thoughts and Notes:

Recipe:

Rating: ☆☆☆☆☆ Difficulty: ☆☆☆☆☆ Prep Time: Cook Time:

Ingredients:

Cooking Instructions:

Thoughts and Notes:

Recipe:

Rating: ☆☆☆☆☆ Difficulty: ✿✿✿✿✿ Prep Time: Cook Time:

Ingredients:

Cooking Instructions:

Thoughts and Notes:

Recipe:

Rating: ☆☆☆☆☆ Difficulty: ☆☆☆☆☆ Prep Time: Cook Time:

Ingredients:

Cooking Instructions:

Thoughts and Notes:

Recipe:

Rating: ☆☆☆☆☆ Difficulty: ☆☆☆☆☆ Prep Time: Cook Time:

Ingredients:

Cooking Instructions:

Thoughts and Notes:

Recipe:

Rating: ☆☆☆☆☆ Difficulty: ✿✿✿✿✿ Prep Time: Cook Time:

Ingredients:

Cooking Instructions:

Thoughts and Notes:

Recipe:

Rating: ☆☆☆☆☆ Difficulty: ☆☆☆☆☆ Prep Time: Cook Time:

Ingredients:

Cooking Instructions:

Thoughts and Notes:

Recipe:

Rating: ☆☆☆☆☆ Difficulty: ☆☆☆☆☆ Prep Time: Cook Time:

Ingredients:

Cooking Instructions:

Thoughts and Notes:

Recipe:

Rating: ☆☆☆☆☆ Difficulty: ☆☆☆☆☆ Prep Time: Cook Time:

Ingredients:

Cooking Instructions:

Thoughts and Notes:

Recipe:

Rating: ☆☆☆☆☆ Difficulty: ☆☆☆☆☆ Prep Time: Cook Time:

Ingredients:

Cooking Instructions:

Thoughts and Notes:

Recipe:

Rating: ☆☆☆☆☆ Difficulty: ☆☆☆☆☆ Prep Time: Cook Time:

Ingredients:

Cooking Instructions:

Thoughts and Notes:

Recipe:

Rating: ☆☆☆☆☆ Difficulty: ☆☆☆☆☆ Prep Time: Cook Time:

Ingredients:

Cooking Instructions:

Thoughts and Notes:

Recipe:

Rating: ☆☆☆☆☆ Difficulty: ☆☆☆☆☆ Prep Time: Cook Time:

Ingredients:

Cooking Instructions:

Thoughts and Notes:

Recipe:

Rating: ☆☆☆☆☆ Difficulty: ✿✿✿✿✿ Prep Time: Cook Time:

Ingredients:

Cooking Instructions:

Thoughts and Notes:

Recipe:

Rating: ☆☆☆☆☆ Difficulty: ✿✿✿✿✿ Prep Time: Cook Time:

Ingredients:

Cooking Instructions:

Thoughts and Notes:

Recipe:

Rating: ☆☆☆☆☆ Difficulty: ☆☆☆☆☆ Prep Time: Cook Time:

Ingredients:

Cooking Instructions:

Thoughts and Notes:

Recipe:

Rating: ☆☆☆☆☆ Difficulty: ☆☆☆☆☆ Prep Time: Cook Time:

Ingredients:

Cooking Instructions:

Thoughts and Notes:

Recipe:

Rating: ☆☆☆☆☆ Difficulty: ☆☆☆☆☆ Prep Time: Cook Time:

Ingredients:

Cooking Instructions:

Thoughts and Notes:

Recipe:

Rating: ☆☆☆☆☆ Difficulty: ☆☆☆☆☆ Prep Time: Cook Time:

Ingredients:

Cooking Instructions:

Thoughts and Notes:

Recipe:

Rating: ☆☆☆☆☆ Difficulty: ☆☆☆☆☆ Prep Time:　　　　　Cook Time:

Ingredients:

Cooking Instructions:

Thoughts and Notes:

Recipe:

Rating: ☆☆☆☆☆ Difficulty: ✿✿✿✿✿ Prep Time: Cook Time:

Ingredients:

Cooking Instructions:

Thoughts and Notes:

Recipe:

Rating: ☆☆☆☆☆ Difficulty: ✿✿✿✿✿ Prep Time: Cook Time:

Ingredients:

Cooking Instructions:

Thoughts and Notes:

Recipe:

Rating: ☆☆☆☆☆ Difficulty: ☆☆☆☆☆ Prep Time: Cook Time:

Ingredients:

Cooking Instructions:

Thoughts and Notes:

Recipe:

Rating: ☆☆☆☆☆ Difficulty: ☆☆☆☆☆ Prep Time: Cook Time:

Ingredients:

Cooking Instructions:

Thoughts and Notes:

Recipe:

Rating: ☆☆☆☆☆ Difficulty: ☆☆☆☆☆ Prep Time: Cook Time:

Ingredients:

Cooking Instructions:

Thoughts and Notes:

Recipe:

Rating: ☆☆☆☆☆ Difficulty: ☆☆☆☆☆ Prep Time: Cook Time:

Ingredients:

Cooking Instructions:

Thoughts and Notes:

Recipe:

Rating: ☆☆☆☆☆ Difficulty: ☆☆☆☆☆ Prep Time: Cook Time:

Ingredients:

Cooking Instructions:

Thoughts and Notes:

Recipe:

Rating: ☆☆☆☆☆ Difficulty: ☆☆☆☆☆ Prep Time: Cook Time:

Ingredients:

Cooking Instructions:

Thoughts and Notes:

Recipe:

Rating: ☆☆☆☆☆ Difficulty: ☆☆☆☆☆ Prep Time:　　　　　Cook Time:

Ingredients:

Cooking Instructions:

Thoughts and Notes:

Recipe:

Rating: ☆☆☆☆☆ Difficulty: ☆☆☆☆☆ Prep Time: Cook Time:

Ingredients:

Cooking Instructions:

Thoughts and Notes:

Recipe:

Rating: ☆☆☆☆☆ Difficulty: ☆☆☆☆☆ Prep Time: Cook Time:

Ingredients:

Cooking Instructions:

Thoughts and Notes:

Recipe:

Rating: ☆☆☆☆☆ Difficulty: ☆☆☆☆☆ Prep Time: Cook Time:

Ingredients:

Cooking Instructions:

Thoughts and Notes:

Recipe:

Rating: ☆☆☆☆☆ Difficulty: ☆☆☆☆☆ Prep Time: Cook Time:

Ingredients:

Cooking Instructions:

Thoughts and Notes:

Recipe:

Rating: ☆☆☆☆☆ Difficulty: ☆☆☆☆☆ Prep Time: 　　　　Cook Time:

Ingredients:

Cooking Instructions:

Thoughts and Notes:

Recipe:

Rating: ☆☆☆☆☆ Difficulty: ✿✿✿✿✿ Prep Time: Cook Time:

Ingredients:

Cooking Instructions:

Thoughts and Notes:

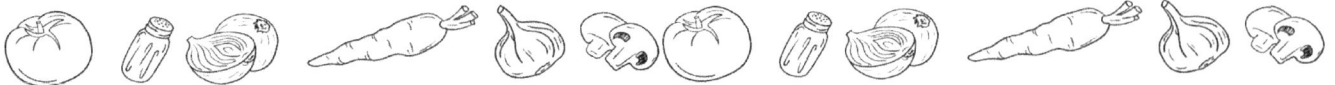

Recipe:

Rating: ☆☆☆☆☆ Difficulty: ☆☆☆☆☆ Prep Time: Cook Time:

Ingredients:

Cooking Instructions:

Thoughts and Notes:

Recipe:

Rating: ☆☆☆☆☆ Difficulty: ✿✿✿✿✿ Prep Time: Cook Time:

Ingredients:

Cooking Instructions:

Thoughts and Notes:

Recipe:

Rating: ☆☆☆☆☆ Difficulty: ✿✿✿✿✿ Prep Time: Cook Time:

Ingredients:

Cooking Instructions:

Thoughts and Notes:

Recipe:

Rating: ☆☆☆☆☆ Difficulty: ☆☆☆☆☆ Prep Time:　　　　Cook Time:

Ingredients:

Cooking Instructions:

Thoughts and Notes:

Recipe:

Rating: ☆☆☆☆☆ Difficulty: ☆☆☆☆☆ Prep Time: Cook Time:

Ingredients:

Cooking Instructions:

Thoughts and Notes:

Recipe:

Rating: ☆☆☆☆☆ Difficulty: ✿✿✿✿✿ Prep Time:　　　　　Cook Time:

Ingredients:

Cooking Instructions:

Thoughts and Notes:

Recipe:

Rating: ☆☆☆☆☆ Difficulty: ☆☆☆☆☆ Prep Time: Cook Time:

Ingredients:

Cooking Instructions:

Thoughts and Notes:

Recipe:

Rating: ☆☆☆☆☆ Difficulty: ☆☆☆☆☆ Prep Time: Cook Time:

Ingredients:

Cooking Instructions:

Thoughts and Notes:

Recipe:

Rating: ☆☆☆☆☆ Difficulty: ☆☆☆☆☆ Prep Time: Cook Time:

Ingredients:

Cooking Instructions:

Thoughts and Notes:

Recipe:

Rating: ☆☆☆☆☆ Difficulty: ✿✿✿✿✿ Prep Time: Cook Time:

Ingredients:

Cooking Instructions:

Thoughts and Notes:

Recipe:

Rating: ☆☆☆☆☆ Difficulty: ☆☆☆☆☆ Prep Time: Cook Time:

Ingredients:

Cooking Instructions:

Thoughts and Notes:

Recipe:

Rating: ☆☆☆☆☆ Difficulty: ☆☆☆☆☆ Prep Time: Cook Time:

Ingredients:

Cooking Instructions:

Thoughts and Notes:

Recipe:

Rating: ☆☆☆☆☆ Difficulty: ✿✿✿✿✿ Prep Time: Cook Time:

Ingredients:

Cooking Instructions:

Thoughts and Notes:

Recipe:

Rating: ☆☆☆☆☆ Difficulty: ✿✿✿✿✿ Prep Time: Cook Time:

Ingredients:

Cooking Instructions:

Thoughts and Notes:

Recipe:

Rating: ☆☆☆☆☆ Difficulty: ✿✿✿✿✿ Prep Time: Cook Time:

Ingredients:

Cooking Instructions:

Thoughts and Notes:

Recipe:

Rating: ☆☆☆☆☆ Difficulty: ✿✿✿✿✿ Prep Time: Cook Time:

Ingredients:

Cooking Instructions:

Thoughts and Notes:

Recipe:

Rating: ☆☆☆☆☆ Difficulty: ☆☆☆☆☆ Prep Time: Cook Time:

Ingredients:

Cooking Instructions:

Thoughts and Notes:

Recipe:

Rating: ☆☆☆☆☆ Difficulty: ✿✿✿✿✿ Prep Time: Cook Time:

Ingredients:

Cooking Instructions:

Thoughts and Notes:

Made in the USA
Middletown, DE
28 February 2022